PRIMARY SOURCE
EXPLORERS

A JOURNEY WITH HENRY HUDSON

LAURA HAMILTON WAXMAN

LERNER PUBLICATIONS ◆ MINNEAPOLIS

*For Mom and Dad, who helped me
navigate the rough waters of life*

Content consultant:
Peter Cooper Mancall, PhD, History,
Harvard University Andrew W. Mellon Professor of the Humanities,
University of Southern California

Lerner Publications Company
A division of Lerner Publishing Group, Inc.
241 First Avenue North
Minneapolis, MN 55401 USA

For reading levels and more information, look up this title at
www.lernerbooks.com.

Main body text set in AvenirLTPro 12/18.
Typeface provided by Linotype AG.

Library of Congress Cataloging-in-Publication Data

Names: Waxman, Laura Hamilton, author.
Title: A journey with Henry Hudson / Laura Hamilton Waxman.
Description: Minneapolis : Lerner Publications, [2016] | Series: Primary
    source explorers | Includes bibliographical references and index. |
    Audience: Grades 4–6.
Identifiers: LCCN 2016009616 (print) | LCCN 2016009782 (ebook) | ISBN
    9781512407747 (lb : alk. paper) | ISBN 9781512410976 (eb pdf)
Subjects: LCSH: Hudson, Henry, –1611—Juvenile literature. | Explorers—
    America—Biography—Juvenile literature. | Explorers—Great
    Britain—Biography—Juvenile literature. | America—Discovery and
    exploration—British—Juvenile literature. | Hudson River Valley (N.Y.
    and N.J.)—Discovery and exploration—Juvenile literature.
Classification: LCC E129.H8 W39 2016 (print) | LCC E129.H8 (ebook) | DDC
    910.92—dc23

LC record available at http://lccn.loc.gov/2016009616

Manufactured in the United States of America
1-39346-21158-11/29/2016

CONTENTS

 = Denotes primary source

INTRODUCTION
A WINDOW INTO THE PAST

Henry Hudson's famous voyages took place in the early seventeenth century. In those days, there were no cameras to record events. No one texted or sent e-mails about their lives. But historians know a lot about Hudson's voyages because they have carefully studied primary sources.

Primary sources are written documents, images, and other objects created when a historical person lived. Some of the

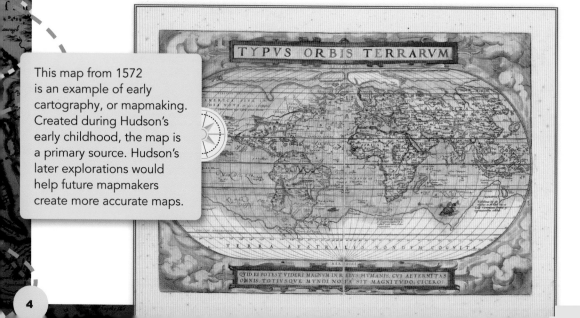

This map from 1572 is an example of early cartography, or mapmaking. Created during Hudson's early childhood, the map is a primary source. Hudson's later explorations would help future mapmakers create more accurate maps.

This engraving of Hudson was made in the nineteenth century, after Hudson lived, so it is not a primary source.

richest primary sources are diaries, letters, and government records. Primary sources can also be maps, artwork, tools, and other artifacts. Together, they provide a firsthand account of what life was like in the past. They help to paint a picture of the thoughts, motivations, and experiences of a person who lived long ago.

Some of Hudson's own writings about his voyages have survived. So have reports written by his crew members. Other records from his era help to fill in the blanks. Such primary sources provide details of Hudson's voyages and the challenges he faced. As you learn about his explorations, you'll be able to read or examine some of those primary sources for yourself.

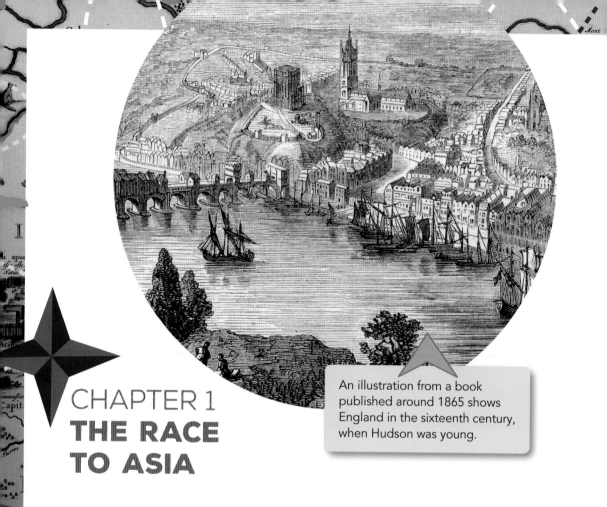

An illustration from a book published around 1865 shows England in the sixteenth century, when Hudson was young.

CHAPTER 1
THE RACE TO ASIA

The early years of Henry Hudson's life are a mystery. No primary sources have been found to tell of his time as a boy, teenager, or young man. But historians believe that he was probably born in England around 1570. As an adult, he knew how to read, write, and take charge of a ship. So historians also figure that he must have had some sort of education and a good amount of training at sea.

EUROPEAN EXPLORATION

At the time young Hudson was learning his ABCs, exploration—especially of North America—was becoming more and more common. Europeans were hungry for more knowledge about Earth and its geography. They had already discovered some valuable lands in the Caribbean and South America. They had also found a sea route to Asia. The route had replaced the more difficult and dangerous land route, called the Silk Road.

A safe route to Asia was very important to Europeans. European traders went to Asia to get valuable goods. These included silk, spices, porcelain, pearls, coffee, and tea. Traders and merchants grew rich selling these goods in Europe.

An artist named Stefano Bonsignori depicted the Silk Road in this piece he created during Hudson's lifetime.

A FASTER PASSAGE TO ASIA?

The sea route to Asia was better than traveling on foot. But that didn't mean it was quick and easy. It involved sailing all the way around Africa. And it took a year or longer each way. Another problem was the Portuguese, who controlled much of Europe's trade with Asia. They claimed this sea route for themselves, attempting to block other European explorers from using it because they were the first to discover it. Pirates also made the southern route to Asia dangerous for European sailors.

   Some Europeans wondered if there was a more direct route. Perhaps they could sail north to the Arctic instead of south around Africa. A ship would have to navigate through icy waters. But Europeans believed that the trip could be shortened to just three months each way.

Pirates were a real danger for European sailors. This work of art showing a raid by pirates was created about twenty years before Hudson was born, but pirates remained a threat in Hudson's era.

Sailors in Hudson's time navigated the seas in ships like these. This image was created in 1901, long after Hudson's death.

HENRY HUDSON ENTERS THE SCENE

England wanted to be the first to find a northern route to Asia. Then its traders would be able to buy and sell Asian goods faster than anyone else. That meant England would control trade with Asia the way Portugal did. Having that kind of control would bring the nation great wealth and power.

But first, the English needed to find a northern route. And they needed to do it before any other country did. They also needed a fearless and experienced sea explorer. They soon set their sights on Henry Hudson.

WHAT DO YOU THINK?

In Hudson's time, European nations placed great importance on wealth and power. Do you think modern nations, such as the United States, have similar values? Why or why not?

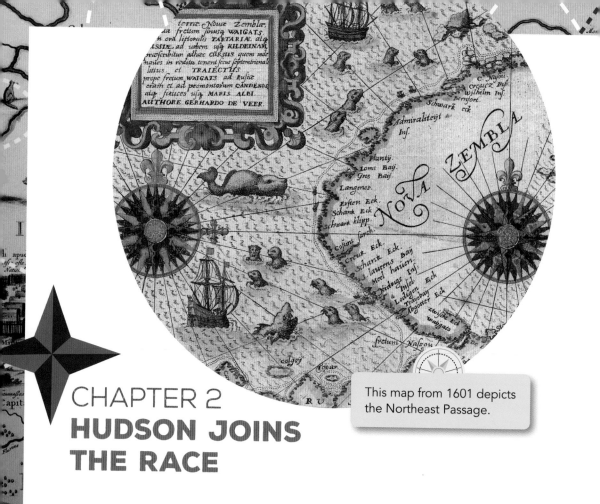

This map from 1601 depicts the Northeast Passage.

CHAPTER 2
HUDSON JOINS THE RACE

In 1607 an English trading company called the Muscovy Company hired Hudson to discover a northern route to Asia. Hudson had two options. He could try to sail northeast, toward Russia. Or he could try to sail northwest, toward North America. The company asked Hudson to go northeast to find what was called the Northeast Passage.

A RISKY VOYAGE

Hudson's plan was to sail northeast until he reached the North Pole. Europeans knew that Arctic waters froze solid in winter. But they incorrectly thought the ice melted in summer. They believed it was possible to sail over the North Pole to Asia in the warmest months.

The Muscovy Company gave Hudson a small ship called the *Hopewell*. It would carry Hudson and about a dozen crew members. Hudson and his crew knew their voyage would be risky. Other explorers had died trying to find a northern route to Asia. But the risks didn't stop Hudson. He was determined to be the first man to find the Northeast Passage.

SETTING SAIL

The *Hopewell* set sail from England on May 1, 1607. By the middle of June, it had reached Greenland. Hudson then headed northeast toward the North Pole. He soon discovered that the Arctic seas did not melt in summer. Instead, he had to steer his ship around huge ice floes. If he wasn't careful, these sheets of floating ice could surround the boat and trap it. Once trapped, the *Hopewell* wouldn't be able to escape. Another danger was icebergs. If one of those hit the ship, the *Hopewell* would be smashed to bits.

These frozen mountains show the North Pole's extreme climate. Hudson knew little about this climate, as the North Pole had not yet been explored in the seventeenth century.

The extreme cold and lack of fresh food also made life on the *Hopewell* unpleasant. The harsh weather wore the crew down. But somehow, Hudson and his crew kept going.

A FAILED ATTEMPT

The farther north Hudson sailed, the more ice he encountered. In late July, a deadly iceberg was heading right toward the *Hopewell*. To escape, Hudson used a small boat kept on the ship. He ordered his men to attach the boat to the *Hopewell*, paddle like crazy, and tow the ship out of harm's way. They escaped from the iceberg just in time. Hudson realized that he couldn't go any farther. The path was just too treacherous. He was forced to return to England empty-handed.

WHAT DO YOU THINK?

Why do you think Hudson and his crew were willing to take such a dangerous voyage? How would England have viewed them if they'd succeeded? What would success have done for Henry Hudson and his men?

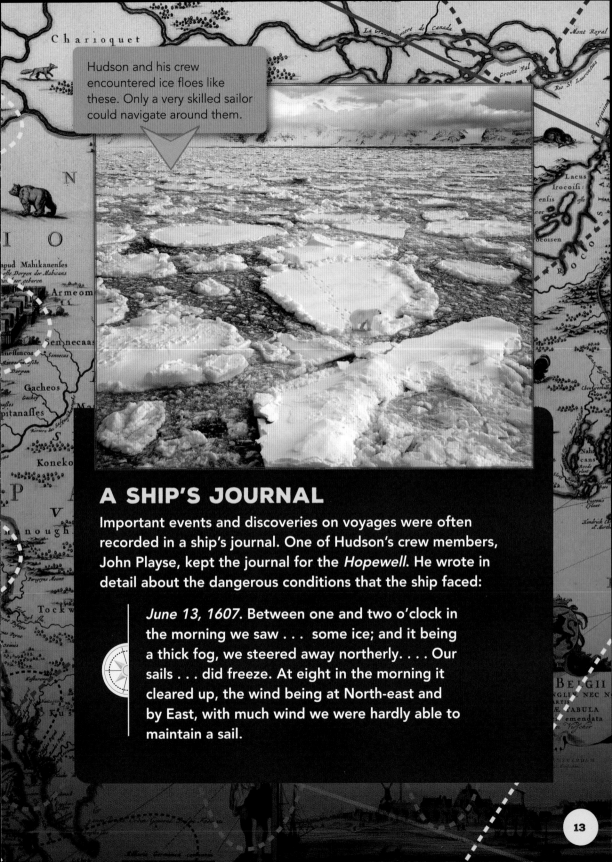

Hudson and his crew encountered ice floes like these. Only a very skilled sailor could navigate around them.

A SHIP'S JOURNAL

Important events and discoveries on voyages were often recorded in a ship's journal. One of Hudson's crew members, John Playse, kept the journal for the *Hopewell*. He wrote in detail about the dangerous conditions that the ship faced:

> *June 13, 1607.* Between one and two o'clock in the morning we saw . . . some ice; and it being a thick fog, we steered away northerly. . . . Our sails . . . did freeze. At eight in the morning it cleared up, the wind being at North-east and by East, with much wind we were hardly able to maintain a sail.

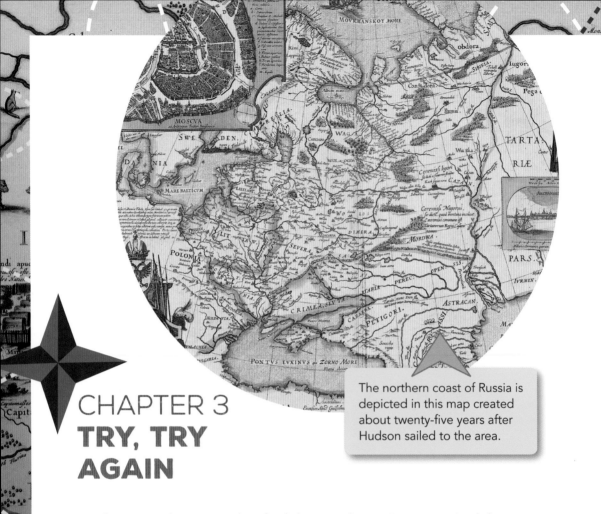

The northern coast of Russia is depicted in this map created about twenty-five years after Hudson sailed to the area.

CHAPTER 3
TRY, TRY AGAIN

Hudson was determined to find the Northeast Passage. And the Muscovy Company was willing to pay him to give it another try. This time, though, he would sail along the northern coast of Russia and then over the North Pole instead of heading to Greenland.

HEADING FOR RUSSIA

Once again, Hudson set sail on the *Hopewell*. He and a crew of fifteen left London on April 22, 1608. The crew included experienced sailors, a carpenter, a cook, and Hudson's teenage son, John. His other two sons, Richard and Oliver, stayed behind with his wife, Katherine.

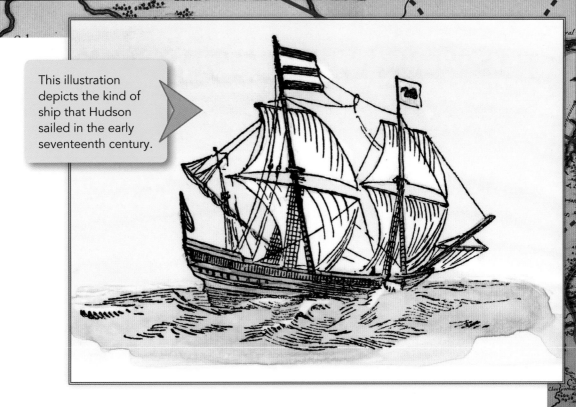

This illustration depicts the kind of ship that Hudson sailed in the early seventeenth century.

For a month, the *Hopewell* sailed northeast toward the northern coast of Russia. On this voyage, Hudson helped to write the ship's journal himself. In early June, he wrote that ice was becoming dangerously thick. One day, the *Hopewell* nearly got trapped in a narrow path between ice floes. "We returned the way we had entered," wrote Hudson, "with a few rubs of our ship against the ice."

BLOCKED BY ICE

Despite the ice, Hudson managed to take the *Hopewell* up to Novaya Zemlya. These islands lie off the northern coast of Russia. At Novaya Zemlya, Hudson searched for a strait between the islands. He hoped this narrow waterway would lead to a passage over the North Pole. But ice blocked every path he tried.

An undated historical map highlights Novaya Zemlya, the islands to which Hudson sailed in 1608.

Hudson refused to give up. At times, that determination put his crew in danger. More than once, ice floes nearly trapped the *Hopewell*. One day in July, ice surrounded them. The crew was forced to grab anything they could to push it away. They used the ship's poles, beams, and anchors to save themselves and their ship.

AN UNHAPPY CREW

Despite these close calls, Hudson kept going. But his crew didn't share his desire to press on. Winter would be coming soon. How would they deal with the freezing seas? Where would they get enough food to survive? To force Hudson's hand, they may have led a mutiny against him. They gave Hudson no choice but to return home.

WHAT DO YOU THINK?

Why do you think Hudson chose to take his teenage son John with him on the Hopewell? Why would he have exposed his son to such great risks?

Hudson may have been overtaken in a mutiny, or a rebellion by his crew, in the year 1608. This illustration depicts a later mutiny involving Hudson, which historians know for a fact took place.

MUTINY AMONG THE CREW?

In a mutiny, the crew takes over a ship from its captain. They may even threaten to kill him. Hudson's own words show that a mutiny likely took place on the *Hopewell* around August 7, 1608:

> I used all diligence to arrive at London and therefore I now gave my company certificate under my hands of my free and willing return, without persuasion or force of any one or more of them.

Hudson is saying that he made a promise to his crew to return to England. He also says that he did it without being forced or harmed. Historians believe he wouldn't have written these words unless his crew *did* force him. Historians think the crew probably made Hudson write those words so it looked as if they had not tried to overtake their captain.

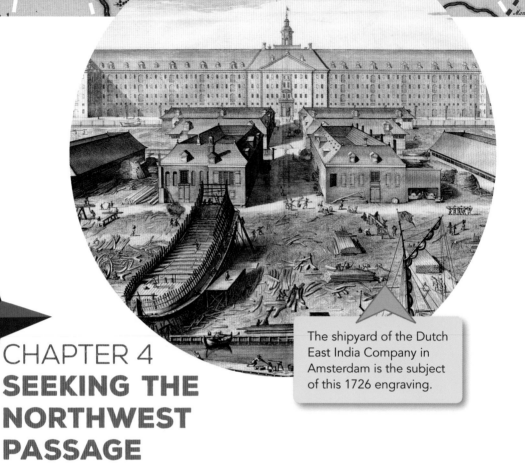

The shipyard of the Dutch East India Company in Amsterdam is the subject of this 1726 engraving.

CHAPTER 4
SEEKING THE NORTHWEST PASSAGE

Hudson was out of luck—and out of work. England's Muscovy Company didn't want to hire him again. But others were interested. After all, Hudson had managed to keep his ship and crew in one piece in the Arctic. And he'd done it not once but twice!

THE DUTCH EAST INDIA COMPANY

The Dutch East India Company in Holland offered to hire him. This powerful company had a lot of money and the full support of the Dutch government. It wanted to find a northern route to Asia before England—or anyone else—did. Then it could control this valuable route for Holland.

The company believed that the Northeast Passage was the best bet. They offered to pay Hudson to give it another chance. Hudson would have rather searched for the Northwest Passage. But he needed the money, so he accepted the offer. He signed a written contract saying that he agreed to sail northeast toward Novaya Zemlya once again. He also agreed that he wouldn't waste time searching for any other route, including the Northwest Passage.

Hudson signs a contract with the Dutch East India Company in this engraving made in 1870.

NEW SHIP, NEW CREW

The Dutch company gave Hudson a small but speedy Dutch ship called the *Half Moon*. The company also provided him with a crew of fifteen to twenty men. On March 25, 1609, they set sail from Holland. They traveled northeast through icy waters. But as Hudson expected, the ice soon blocked them. Meanwhile, Hudson's crew was cold and miserable. Some of them wanted to give up. They may have even threatened to turn against Hudson in another mutiny. Hudson suggested that they change course. Why not head west in search of a Northwest Passage instead?

The *Half Moon* is shown in this image created long after Hudson's 1609 journey.

Two Mi'kmaw Indians paddle a birchbark canoe in this eighteenth-century watercolor.

DISOBEYING ORDERS

Hudson's plan meant breaking his contract with the Dutch East India Company. But he and his crew decided to take the risk. They sailed across the Atlantic Ocean and then south to Maine. There they stopped to collect fresh drinking water, lobsters, and fish. They also traded with American Indians in the area, who may have been part of the Mi'kmaw people. These men and women were used to exchanging goods with fur traders from France. They were friendly toward Hudson and eager to trade. But Hudson's men had had little experience with American Indians. His crew feared and distrusted them.

On July 24, some of Hudson's crew decided to raid an American Indian village. They stole their supplies, including a small boat. Then they quickly sailed south before anyone came after them. Eventually they turned north again and headed toward modern-day New York. Hudson had heard that a possible route to the Northwest Passage might be found there. In early September, they entered New York Harbor. They began exploring it for an entrance to the Northwest Passage.

ENCOUNTERING AMERICAN INDIANS

While the crew explored, American Indians came to them in canoes. These were likely members of the Canarsie people. Most were warm and friendly. They wanted to trade with Hudson. But a small number of American Indians attacked the *Half Moon*. These men may have belonged to the Lenape people.

Europeans interact with the Lenape in an engraving from 1702.

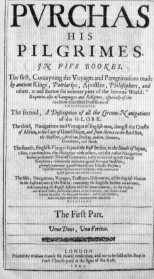

EUROPEAN TRADE WITH AMERICAN INDIANS

Hudson's second-in-command was an Englishman named Robert Juet. Juet kept the ship's journal for the voyage. He wrote about what it was like to trade with American Indians in New York Harbor:

> [They] brought green tobacco and gave it to us for knives and beads. They go in deer skins loose, well dressed. They have yellow copper [brass]. They desire clothes and are very civil. They have great store of maize or Indian wheat, whereof they make good bread.

Primary source writings like these tell historians a lot about the items that American Indians and Europeans valued.

The attackers killed one of Hudson's men and wounded two others. Three days later, Hudson's men kidnapped some American Indians who had come on their ship to trade. This kidnapping was possibly a warning to other American Indians. Hudson's crew didn't want to be attacked again.

SAILING THE HUDSON RIVER

By then Hudson had decided to travel up the deepest river leading out of New York Harbor. It would later be named the Hudson River. Hudson was not the first European to discover the Hudson River. But he was the first to sail up it. He hoped it would lead west across the continent to the Pacific Ocean.

The Hudson River appears in a map from around the year 1630.

From there he thought he could sail west to Asia. But he soon discovered that the upper part of the river grew too shallow to sail. He was forced to turn around and return to the harbor.

Along the way, the *Half Moon* had had many pleasant encounters with American Indians. But on October 2, two canoes full of men shot arrows at them. Hudson's crew shot back and killed several American Indians. Two days later, the *Half Moon* was on its way back to Europe. Once again, Hudson had nothing to show for his travels.

WHAT DO YOU THINK?

Why do you think Hudson and his crew decided to seek the Northwest Passage against their orders from Holland? Why didn't they simply return to Europe?

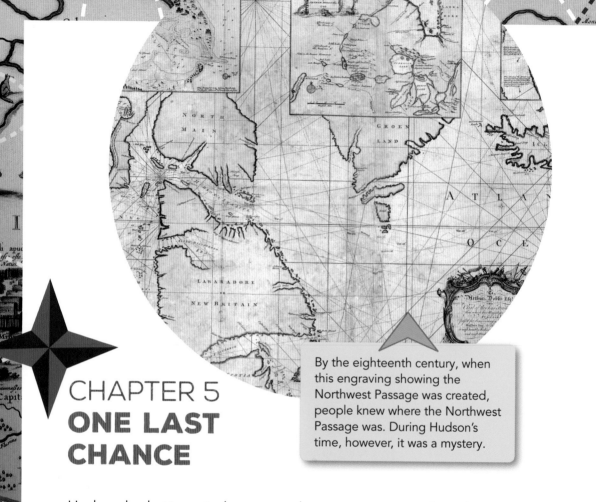

By the eighteenth century, when this engraving showing the Northwest Passage was created, people knew where the Northwest Passage was. During Hudson's time, however, it was a mystery.

CHAPTER 5
ONE LAST CHANCE

Hudson had attempted more northern sea routes to Asia than any other explorer. He'd failed so far, but he was sure he could find the Northwest Passage. He just needed another chance. Luckily for him, a few members of England's Muscovy Company agreed to hire him. This time, Hudson was going to try entering North American waters from much farther north than New York Harbor.

FIERCE WATERS

Hudson set sail on April 17, 1610. His small ship was called the *Discovery*. It held a crew of about twenty men and two ship's boys. One of those boys was Hudson's son John. Hudson steered the ship northwest to northeast Canada. There he began to navigate through a dangerous strait that would later be known as the Hudson Strait. It had a fast current and swirling waters. It also had what looked to the men like mountains of deadly ice.

The cliffside of Akpatok Island stands tall near the entrance of the Hudson Strait.

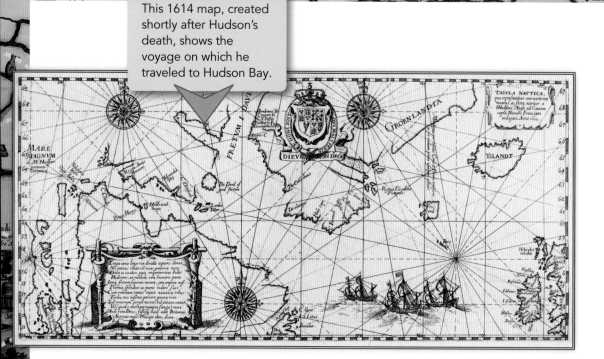

This 1614 map, created shortly after Hudson's death, shows the voyage on which he traveled to Hudson Bay.

Hudson steered his boat 300 miles (482 kilometers) into the strait. Eventually he entered a quieter bay. That bay later became known as Hudson Bay. Hudson believed he would find an entrance to the Northwest Passage there. He sailed the entire length of the bay and even explored James Bay, Canada, to the south. Back and forth he went, searching and searching for weeks on end. During this time, his crew grew frightened and angry. Fall was coming. How could they make it back to England before winter set in?

Hudson's crew began complaining about him behind his back. Hudson disciplined some of them for being disloyal. But that didn't help. His crew grew even angrier, especially when frozen ice trapped them in James Bay that November. They would have to spend the harsh winter on land and hope they somehow survived.

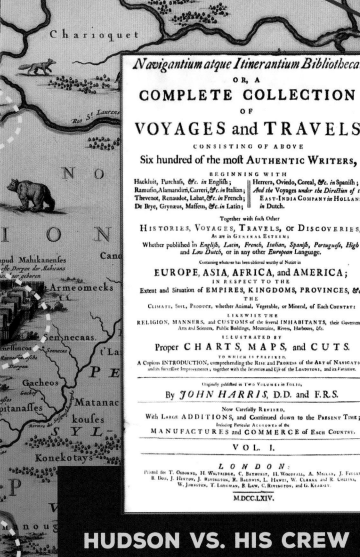

Abacuk Prickett's words, captured in this volume, are an excellent resource for those wanting to learn more about Hudson's explorations.

HUDSON VS. HIS CREW

One of Hudson's crew members was named Abacuk Prickett. He kept his own journal of the *Discovery*'s voyage. Prickett writes that Hudson "was in despair" of ever finding the Northwest Passage. Yet Hudson didn't let those negative feelings stop him. He wanted to keep searching for the Northwest Passage no matter what. His crew didn't feel the same. Prickett wrote, "There was one [crew member] who told the Master that if he had a hundred pounds, he would give fourscore and ten [ninety] to be home." This primary source gives us a small window into the thoughts and emotions of Hudson and his crew.

A LONG, CRUEL WINTER

The cruel Canadian winter was almost too much to bear. To make matters worse, the crew didn't have enough food. They were starving and sick with scurvy. In spring a member of the Cree people approached them. He traded meat and warm animal skins for an axe. But he didn't seem to trust Hudson, and he didn't return.

Scurvy, caused by a lack of vitamin C, was once a serious health concern for anyone who spent extended time at sea. This painting shows sea travelers reaching for fruit rich in vitamin C.

GREENLAND
(DENMARK)

Greenland
Sea

Nordcapp
(North Cape)

BAFFIN
ISLAND

Davis Strait

Denmark Strait

ICELAND

Norwegian
Sea

SWEDEN

FINLAND

Hudson Bay

LABRADOR

Labrador
Sea

NORTH
ATLANTIC
OCEAN

FAROE ISLANDS

ORKNEY
ISLANDS

NORWAY

North
Sea

UNITED
KINGDOM

NORTH AMERICA

James
Bay

IRELAND

London
★

★Amsterdam
NETHERLANDS

EUROPE

NEWFOUNDLAND

FRANCE

ITALY

Albany,
NY

NOVA
SCOTIA

SABLE
ISLAND

PORTUGAL

SPAIN

AFRICA

**HENRY HUDSON'S
FINAL TWO JOURNEYS**

By June the ice in the bay began to break up. Hudson took the ship's small boat and a few men to search for more Cree. He hoped to buy food and supplies. But the Cree were frightened of the European strangers. They set trees on fire close to shore to scare them off.

MUTINY!

While Hudson was away, some of his men planned a mutiny. They knew that Hudson was determined to keep searching for the Northwest Passage. His men were just as determined to go home.

On June 22, most of the crew turned against Hudson. They tied his arms behind his back and forced him onto the ship's small boat. They also forced out his son John and seven sick crew members. Then the crew sailed away on the *Discovery* and returned to England. Hudson was left with no food or supplies in the icy bay. He and the others likely died there. They were never seen or heard from again.

REMEMBERING HENRY HUDSON

Henry Hudson never did find a northern route to Asia. In fact, no one would find and sail the Northwest Passage until 1906.

This work of art shows Hudson abandoned by his crew.

The Hudson River, shown here, is an important part of Henry Hudson's legacy.

But Hudson's explorations gave Europeans of his era a better understanding of Earth's geography. His travels to North America also set the stage for European trade and settlements in Canada, New York, and New Jersey. And his powerful determination inspired the explorers who came after him.

WHAT DO YOU THINK?

Hudson's explorations inspired Europeans to come to Canada, New York, and New Jersey. At first, they benefited from a booming fur trade. Over time, they began to live permanently in the area. How do you think these changes affected the American Indians living in these areas?

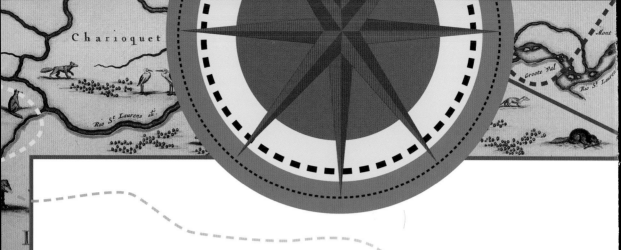

TIMELINE

1570 Henry Hudson is born in England around this time.

1607 On May 1, Hudson sets out from England on the *Hopewell* in search of the Northeast Passage. On September 15, he returns to England empty-handed.

1608 On April 22, Hudson leaves on the *Hopewell* for a second voyage to find the Northeast Passage. He returns to England without success in late August.

1609 In January the Dutch East India Company hires Hudson to find the Northeast Passage. On March 25, Hudson sets sail from Holland on the *Half Moon*. About two months later, he and his crew decide to sail west to find the Northwest Passage. In early September, the *Half Moon* begins sailing up the Hudson River. The *Half Moon* ends up returning to Europe in November.

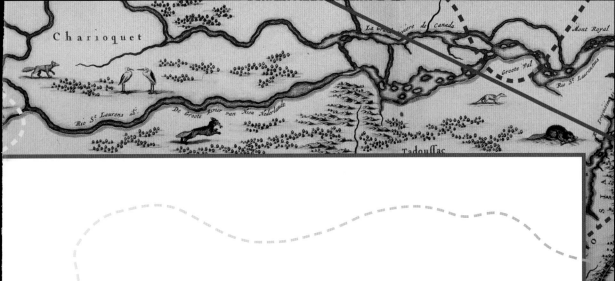

■■■ **1610** On April 17, Hudson sails the *Discovery* from England to Canada in search of the Northwest Passage. In late June, the *Discovery* enters the Hudson Strait. The *Discovery* is trapped by frozen sea ice in James Bay in November. Hudson and his crew barely survive the long Canadian winter.

■■■ **1611** In early June, the ice in the bay begins to break up. Hudson wants to continue searching for the Northwest Passage. On June 22, the crew of the *Discovery* turns against Hudson in a mutiny. They leave him, his son, and seven sick crew members to die in a small boat.

■■■ **1906** Norwegian explorer Roald Amundsen is the first explorer to sail the entire Northwest Passage.

SOURCE NOTES

13 Corey Sandler, *Henry Hudson: Dreams and Obsession* (New York: Citadel, 2007), 46–47.

15 Ibid., 110.

17 Ibid., 119.

23 Robert Juet, "Juet's Journal of Hudson's 1609 Voyage," in Henry Hudson's Voyages by Samuel Purchas (Ann Arbor, MI: University Microfilms, 1966), 592, first published 1625 by Henrie Fetherstone, transcription by Brea Barthel, available online at New Netherland Museum, http://halfmoon.mus.ny.us/Juets-journal.pdf.

29 Sandler, *Henry Hudson*, 265.

29 Ibid., 266.

GLOSSARY

Arctic: of or relating to the North Pole or the region near it

artifact: something created by humans, usually for a practical purpose

bay: an inlet of the sea or other body of water

era: a period of time that is associated with a particular quality, event, or person

iceberg: a very large piece of ice floating in the ocean

ice floe: a usually large, flat, free mass of floating sea ice

merchant: someone who buys and sells goods

mutiny: a situation in which sailors refuse to obey orders and try to take control away from the person who commands them

navigate: to find the way to get to a place when you are traveling

porcelain: a hard, white substance that is very delicate and that is made by baking clay

scurvy: a disease that is caused by not eating enough fruits or vegetables that contain vitamin C

strait: a narrow passage of water that connects two large bodies of water

SELECTED BIBLIOGRAPHY

Chadwick, Ian. *The Life and Voyages of Henry Hudson*. Accessed February 15, 2016. http://www.ianchadwick.com/hudson/.

Hunter, Douglas. *Half Moon: Henry Hudson and the Voyage That Redrew the Map of the New World*. New York: Bloomsbury, 2009.

Juet, Robert. "Juet's Journal of Hudson's 1609 Voyage." New Netherland Museum. Accessed February 15, 2016. http://halfmoon.mus.ny.us/Juets-journal.pdf.

Mancall, Peter C. *Fatal Journey: The Final Expedition of Henry Hudson—a Tale of Mutiny and Murder in the Arctic*. New York: Basic Books, 2009.

Sandler, Corey. *Henry Hudson: Dreams and Obsession*. New York: Citadel, 2007.

Stark, Charlie. "The Twin Mysteries of Henry Hudson—His 1609 Voyage." *Hudson River Valley Review* 25, no. 2 (Spring 2009): 98–106. http://www.hudsonrivervalley.org/review/pdfs/hrvr25pt2online.pdf.

FURTHER INFORMATION

The Age of Discovery
http://exploration.marinersmuseum.org/type/age-of-discovery
Learn about the explorers, ships, and tools of Henry Hudson's era in history.

Enchanted Learning: Explorers from the 1600s
http://www.zoomschool.com/explorers/1600.shtml
Read brief biographies of prominent explorers from Henry Hudson's time, including Hudson himself.

Gould, Jane H. *Henry Hudson*. New York: PowerKids, 2013. This short graphic novel takes you right into Henry Hudson's world.

Kallen, Stuart A. *A Journey with Francisco Vázquez de Coronado*. Minneapolis: Lerner Publications, 2018. Read about another famous explorer and his fascinating travels.

Rogers, Stan. *Northwest Passage*. Toronto: Groundwood Books, 2013. Learn about the different explorers who attempted to discover and sail the Northwest Passage.

LERNER

SOURCE

Expand learning beyond the printed book. Download free, complementary educational resources for this book from our website, www.lerneresource.com.

INDEX

PHOTO ACKNOWLEDGMENTS

The images in this book are used with the permission of: © Memory of the Netherlands/Wikimedia Commons (Public Domain) (map backgrounds); © Historic Map Works/Getty Images, p. 4; The Granger Collection, New York, pp. 5, 7, 8, 19, 22; © Classic Image/Alamy, p. 6; © Classic Image/Alamy, p. 9; © CPC Collection/Alamy, p. 10; © Jose Luis Stephens/Alamy, p. 11; © Moment RF/Getty Images, p. 12; © Steve Allen/Getty Images, p. 13; © DeAgostini/Getty Images, p. 14; © North Wind Picture Archives/Alamy, pp. 15, 24; © Duncan Walker/ Getty Images, p. 16; © Timewatch Images/Alamy, p. 17; © Stadsarchief AmsterdamWikimedia Commons, p. 18; Art and Picture Collection, The New York Public Library. *The Half Moon in the Hudson*, p. 20; © Christie's Images/Bridgeman Images, p. 21; © Berger Collection/ Wikimedia Commons (Public Domain), p. 23; © British Library Board/ Bridgeman Images, p. 26; © Olivier Goujon/SuperStock, p. 27; © AF Fotografie/Alamy, p. 28; Internet Archive Book Images/flickr. com, p. 29; © National Geographic Creative/Alamy, p. 30; © Laura Westlund/Independent Picture Service, p. 31; © Ipsumpix/Corbis/ Getty Images, p. 32; © SuperStock, p. 33.

Front cover: © Look and Learn/Bridgeman Images; © Memory of the Netherlands/Wikimedia Commons (public domain) (map).